My Year of Inspiration

Willie Marrero-LaBonne

Copyright 2011 © Willie Marrero-LaBonne
Willie's Wisdom is a trademark of WisFit, LLC

Cover Design & Illustrations by Kimb Tiboni
and Kimb Manson Graphic Design

Photograph by Jon Recana

All rights reserved. No part of this book may be reproduced or transmitted in any form or by any means, electronic or mechanical, including photocopy, recording, or by any information storage and retrieval system without permission in writing from the author.

ISBN-10: 1467968838

ISBN-13: 978-1467968836

My Year of Inspiration

52 Weeks of Willie's Wisdom

Willie Marrero-LaBonne

Also by Willie Marrero-LaBonne
The Gratitude Book Project: Celebrating 365 Days of Gratitude
(contributing author)

Coming in February 2012
You As God: Awakening the Power Within

My Year of Inspiration

52 Weeks of Willie's Wisdom

Willie Marrero-LaBonne

DEDICATION

To You,
because you are my teacher as we walk this Earth together.

ACKNOWLEDGMENTS

Jay: thank you for being my rock and support throughout the years. You have kept me grounded and because of you I am a better person each and every day.

Brandon: thank you for being my master and my mentor. Your wisdom of ages is really one of the most amazing talents I have seen and experienced. I am honored to be your mother.

Thank you to all the athletes I coached throughout the years. You have always inspired me and because of you I learned to see the greatness in all people. I truly hope that you have realized all of your dreams.

Willie Marrero-LaBonne

CONTENTS

	Dedication	vi
	Acknowledgement	vii
	Introduction	xi
1	Gratitude	1
2	Love	6
3	Acceptance	11
4	Attitude	16
5	Fearless	21
6	Creativity	26
7	Health & Fitness	31
8	Action	36
9	Abundance	41
10	Will power	46
11	Self-Image	51
12	Opportunity	56
13	Awareness	61

Willie Marrero-LaBonne

Introduction

During one starry night when I was five years old, living in a farm in the mountains of Puerto Rico, I looked up at the sky and asked "Where's my wisdom going to come from?" From that moment on it has been my life quest to attain this wisdom. I have read thousands of books on every subject imaginable and continue reading and learning today and every day. When I was younger it was like an addiction, I needed to know how things worked, how things were created, who created what, what people believed in, what made them do the things they do. I have studied hundreds of religions, metaphysical science, quantum physics, molecular biology, witchcraft, and shamanism. What I have come to realize is that things have been the same for centuries. What was once believed - then proved wrong, has come full circle and we believe in it again.

All religions have a common thread and the knowledge and wisdom of ages has always been here and available to all. I have also realized that religion is a way of life, it exists in your heart, not in a temple, not in a doctrine, not in "rules that must be followed." A religion that separates people instead of uniting them is not what God stands for.

I realized that we are immortal and whatever years we spend on this Earth, is nothing but a brief pause in immortality. I have seen the matrix that holds everything together, which is the energy of our true Source, the Universe, the Great Spirit, God, or whatever you choose to call it. I have felt my energy expand and transcend continents to help heal someone who is sick. I have also experience transcendence myself where I have communicated with trees and nature without words and without thoughts.

This is not a fantasy, but it is what is real for me and what I experience daily. I am also very human, get mad, frustrated, and make mistakes. Because I have been so fortunate in all that I have experienced, I wanted to share some thoughts that have helped me navigate through the waters of my life and have found to give me peace, comfort and stability in a world that sometimes is perceived as not so stable.

I hope that what I share here gives you hope, peace and love to continue in your journey and in the realization of your dreams. Know that we are connected and that I am here to bring love and peace to anyone who wants to share these gifts. It is my vision that you realize how wonderful and great you truly are so you too can start sharing your gifts and talents with others.

This booklet is designed to be used as a weekly inspirational guide in your journey to help you find your own wisdom. You can read the weekly message on Sunday night or Monday morning. You can make a copy or write it down on another piece of paper and carry it with you in your wallet so you can read the weekly message every day for the rest the week. Because your subconscious mind is so powerful, by reading and paying attention to these weekly messages on a daily basis, you will start acquiring these messages into your conscious mind and will start actually living the messages in this book. As Jesus said, "The word becomes the flesh." When you read and keep these messages in your mind (give attention), you embody them and they become a part of you.

Because you purchased this book, you can receive a free daily journal to help you get your own ideas on paper as you go through this journey. You can go to www.willielabonne.com to download your copy so you can start using it right away. You can also find a sample of a one week's daily and weekly journal at the end of this book. You can make copies and use it this way too. I have started a blog, where you can leave ideas, comments, or ask questions at http://willieswisdom.blogspot.com

I truly hope that this book helps you remember what an incredible being you truly are, and I hope that your life is filled with peace, love, and abundance throughout your journey.

To your power, magnificence, and divinity with peace and love always,

Willie

Willie Marrero-LaBonne

Section 1

Gratitude

Gratitude - Week 1

Develop an attitude of gratitude, and give thanks for everything that happens to you, knowing that every step forward is a step toward achieving something bigger and better than your current situation.
- Brian Tracy

No matter what is going on your life right now, you have the choice of seeing the glass half empty or half full. In accordance with the Law of Transmutation, everything is always changing. This means that whatever situation you are going through right now, is also changing right now. "Good" or "bad" situation, it doesn't matter because it's only temporary.

The right approach is to enjoy and be grateful for the "good" in your life right now. It is also very important that you appreciate the "bad" because you are learning, becoming stronger, and growing from the challenges. Just know that at the end of the day, it's all good. Trust that you are taken care of, enjoy the journey, and appreciate yourself and everyone in your life.

Gratitude - Week 2

In our daily lives, we must see that it is not happiness that makes us grateful, but the gratefulness that makes us happy.
- Albert Clarke

When you realize that everything that you need you already have, you realize that you have tons to be grateful for. Sometimes we think we need many things, but when we really cut through the smoky mirrors, we realize that everything that's needed we already have. Being grateful for what we have right now opens the doors to more abundance, prosperity, and a richer life. How can the Universe give you more if you are not grateful for what you have right now?

Being happy and grateful for everything that's available to you right now activates the Law of Attraction to bring you even more of everything that makes you feel grateful and happy.

What are you waiting for? Give thanks for everything today and every day, and see how even greater things start showing up in your life.

Gratitude - Week 3

We're so busy watching out for what's just ahead of us that we don't take time to enjoy where we are.
- *Calvin & Hobbes*

Most people live their lives always preparing for the future, thinking about the future, planning for the future. Think about this for a second- Tomorrow is not promised to anyone. Living your life preparing and in fear of what the future holds robs you of the present time, which is all you really have.

This week try to live your life in the present. When plans and worries about the future enter your mind, acknowledge the thought, but come back to placing your attention to what is right now. Live today by being the best version of yourself. Claim the power of the present; live and enjoy what has been given to you.

You can live tomorrow tomorrow by living today today.

Gratitude- Week 4

We often take for granted the very things that most deserve our gratitude.
- Cynthia Ozick

Our society has taught us that we must place value on the transitional and material things. We have forgotten that the real valuable things are the ones that we cannot replace with money: our health, our time with our families and friends, our enjoyment of our lives right now. These are the things that are truly irreplaceable; yet, we choose to over work and value the things that we have acquired with money. Sacrificing the irreplaceable things in our lives results in regret and anxiety when we lose them.

Why wait until something is gone to show your appreciation? Start showing appreciation to your own self and the people in your life which could never be replaced by anything else. Doing this daily will generate a true life experience that will stay with you for the rest of your life.

Live right now without regrets or doubt.

Love - Week 5

Eventually you will come to understand that love heals everything, and love is all there is.
- Gary Zukav

Love is the greatest emotion and feeling in the Universe. When true love is present, it is impossible to hate or condemn anyone. Love makes you feel light and true. When you're in love, it feels like anything is possible. Love gives you wings to fly.

Think about all the people you truly love in your life and this week make a special effort to show this love for everyone - not with material things, but by being there - by acknowledging that they truly mean something special to you and that they are truly loved.

This week share and let your love shine! I guarantee that the whole world will notice it! There's no force stronger than love.

Love - Week 6

Love is like an hourglass, with the heart filling up as the brain empties.
- Jules Renard

To feel true love is not to analyze the feeling or emotion; is not to judge or criticize. To feel love one must find it in the heart while opening it for the world to see. When one comes from love, compassion and freedom reign. When one comes from love, the brain doesn't engage and happiness blossoms. Labels and expectations can be shed if only we come from love. When we come from love, we can finally find peace.

This week keep your attention in love and see the miracles happening all around you.

Love- Week 7

One cannot give what he does not possess. To give love you must possess love. To love others you must love yourself.
- Lee Buscaglia

Without loving yourself first, it's impossible to give true love to others. Loving and appreciating oneself is something that is not taught in our society, yet is one of the first skills that should be learned. By loving and appreciating ourselves we open the doors for more love and appreciation to flow out of ourselves and into others. These doors also remain open for even more love to flow back to us.

Remember that when things are appreciated, they increase in value. Apply this rule to your life. Love and appreciate yourself first and share and give this appreciation to others around you. Remember that the whole world is but a mirror of you - what you see and feel inside is also what you see and feel outside. Realize that YOU have value and are here to share your gifts with the world.

This week take the time to love and appreciate everything that's available in you to share with others.

Love - Week 8

Your task is not to seek for love, but merely to seek and find all the barriers within yourself that you have built against it.
— *Rumi*

Our society teaches that we are separate from one another, yet one man cannot survive by himself. The realization that we are all one and that whatever I do to my neighbor I do to myself is something that is taking too many years for us to remember. This separation mentality is nothing but an illusion and is causing tremendous turmoil around the world. The only way that we can change this paradigm is by changing ourselves, one person at a time.

We must find the barriers that we have built around us and around our lives to keep us separate and bring them down. It's time to tear down the walls and spread love and understanding. It's time to find our own peace and love within so we can share them in order to find love and peace all over the rest of the world.

My Year Of Inspiration

Section 3

Acceptance

Acceptance - Week 9

Arguing with reality is like trying to teach a cat to bark - hopeless.
- Byron Katie

Acceptance of what is, without labels and expectations can make our lives so much easier and stress free. Allowing what is and accepting that everything happens for a reason will save you so much heart ache!

Taking responsibility for what is happening in our lives, knowing that everything is always in motion and everything is always changing, gives us a sense of peace because we know that there's a time for everything. Nature does not rush winter to get to spring; it just waits until the right time, knowing that it is coming.

Enjoy life; accept the challenges and grow from them. Don't rush it… Everything's just right…

Acceptance- Week 10

Everything that has a beginning has an ending. Make your peace with that and all will be well.
― Buddha

Life without death has no meaning. Acceptance of death as a natural part of the life's cycle makes life sweeter. Knowing that you are an eternal being places things into perspective and makes fear of death obsolete. The attachment to this life is something that is taught at an early age. We fear death like is the worst thing that could ever happen. Life and death are just transitional. This is just an experience we are having in this world; just a moment in the eternal time.

This week try to look at your life as an opportunity to share your gifts and talents with the world. It's a blessing to be here today with family and friends.

It's a miracle to be so blessed!

Acceptance - Week 11

The resistance to the unpleasant situation is the root of suffering.
- Baba Ram Dass

The labels and judgment that we place in our situations make our lives miserable. The expectations that we have been taught to have since childhood, combined with the attachments to the outcomes, are the main causes of suffering, anxiety and depression. Knowing that by law, everything is always changing, and that every situation, no matter how difficult it seems, it's always temporary, help us to live our life with peace and surrender.

Resisting change, whether "good" or "bad" is going against life and against the laws of the Universe. You were brought here to grow, learn, and evolve - to become the best version of yourself.

It is time to embrace the challenges, let go of resistance, and trust that you are where you are supposed to be right now: growing and evolving.

Acceptance - Week 12

Your failures won't hurt you until you start blaming them on others.
– Unknown

Everything that has happened and is happening in your life is 100% your responsibility. For some people this is hard to grasp, since our society teaches that we are a product of our environment and our genes. We have complete control of our lives in each and every moment.

We have choices every second of our lives.

How willing we are to accept responsibility for each and every choice we make (and will make) is the catalyst that ignites the freedom and peace in your life right now. The past is gone. Learn from the lessons given and move on- the excess baggage is too heavy for you to carry around. The future is not here yet, stop worrying and predicting the horror movie of your future, which is not even here yet. The now is all you have - claim your power for every decision you make and appreciate that you are the architect of your destiny.

Blame no one!

Section 4

Attitude

Attitude- Week 13

It is not the experiences of your life that determine your outcome. It is the meaning you attach to each experience.
- *Jim Hartness*

Have you noticed how some people are able to rise from a failure like a phoenix rising from the ashes? How about the people who let one failure dictate the course of the rest of their lives? Failures actually have the seeds of success imbedded in them. They are necessary for our growth; they reveal character, and make success that much sweeter.

Thomas Edison "failed" 999 times before he invented the light bulb. When asked how it felt to fail that many times, he said *"I did not fail---I just learn 999 ways on how not to make a light bulb."* When you start putting blame on others- the economy, your mother, your genes, etc. - you lose your power- When you give up your power failure dominates your life. Changing failure into success is achieved by finding what is good about your situation right now.

Your attitude towards the situation makes all the difference!

Attitude- Week 14

Others' attitudes rub off on us, and it's impossible to maintain an upbeat, affirmative attitude if you are constantly around people who are the opposite.
- David Lawrence Prest

It is extremely difficult to maintain a positive attitude when you are surrounded by complainers and whiners. This is the moment when you have to decide if you want to pull away from mediocrity and self-sabotage, or stay and just live while wallowing in your misery.

You alone control your attitude and your feelings towards your situations and your life in general. Surrounding yourself with people who are positive, want to improve themselves, and are all about sharing and helping each other will catapult you towards the realization of your dreams. Toxic relationships, no matter who they are to you, will drag you down eventually suffocating your dreams.

What are you choosing today?

Attitude- Week 15

You're not stuck where you are unless you decide to be.
- Dr Wayne Dyer

So many people think that they are stuck in a situation in their lives. The truth is that since everything in the universe is always changing and evolving, if we feel like we are stuck, we are actually going backwards. When unpleasant situations arise, we must make up our mind to change our attitude and our circumstances.

Everything is just a decision away. We get what we think about most of the time: our wishes and our fears. Wherever your attention is, that's where everything in our lives is. Place your attention where you want to be, not where you don't want to be - and your situation will change.

It is really that simple.

Attitude- Week 16

Write on your heart that every day is the best day of the year.
- Ralph Waldo Emerson

Approaching life with a sense of wonder and the expectation of miracles will provide indeed miracles every day of your life. If there's no attachment and no expectation, everything is a gift. Knowing what you want in life while at the same time releasing the attachment will make all your dreams come true. Trusting that your Source knows exactly what you want and that you are always provided for is having true faith.

Faith is believing before seeing.

This week is all about believing in miracles and knowing that the best of everything is given to you as you allow it to come forth.

Section 5

Fearless

Fearless- Week 17

Face your worry and see it as an illusion. It cannot exist unless you give it power and give it life.
- Robert Anthony

Fear only exists in our minds. Fear can never hurt you unless you give it power. The opposite of fear is not courage, is love.

When love takes over, there cannot be any fear.

What fears are you facing right now? Are they really fears or just your ego trying to protect you? We must face our fears in order to conquer them- it's the only way to get pass the obstacles in the journey of our lives. Success is here!

This week acknowledge your fears and face them head on knowing that these fears are only illusions. Ask, "What's the worst that can happen and can I live with it?"

Reclaim your power today!

Fearless- Week 18

Worry is like a rocking chair - it gives you something to do, but it doesn't get you anywhere.
- Dorothy Galyean

Worrying about this or that can ruin you living the present. Most of the time, whatever we worry about the most is usually not as bad as we perceive it. We bind ourselves to be less than our dreams because we worry about what others may think while doubting our greatness. If you truly believe that you were created in the image of God, don't you think that success is what you should be experiencing?

The love of our Creator is always ever present and is what can carry us in times of darkness and in times of fear and desperation. Let go of fear, if you cannot handle it, give it to someone who can: our Source and Creator. He knows exactly what to do with it so you can get on living the life you are supposed to live today.

From this week forward- Fear no more!

Fearless- Week 19

Too many of us are not living our dreams because we are living our fears.
- Les Brown

Are your dreams on hold because of fears of the future? Fear of not having enough money, fear of not being accepted by your spouse, friends and society, fear of failure, fear of success, fear of what the future or the unknown may hold.

Fear is nothing but an illusion that carries pain and suffering. Fear is the jailer that keeps you prisoner from the person you are meant to be.

How can you soar like the eagle if you let the shackles of fear hold you down? Make the decision to break free from the fear of the future and see how far you can soar.

Living your dreams now is your birthright!

Fearless- Week 20

Fear is that little darkroom where negatives are developed.
- Michael Pritchard

Knowing that you can change the way you feel: your emotions and your attitude, is one of the biggest attributes given to you. Reclaiming this power is your responsibility in order to be able to change your feelings and emotions for the better. You don't have to go from mad to happy in an instant, but shifting your mad (dam backwards) feelings to something softer and lighter, can get you on your way out of feeling so negative about whatever is that you're mad about.

You always have a choice.

Being aware of your choices is the first step in taking control of your fear and your negativity. The power to change negative into positive is always within you.

Start using this power today!

Section 6

Creativity

Creativity- Week 21

Creativity is inventing, experimenting, growing, taking risks, breaking rules, making mistakes, and having fun.
- Mary Lou Cook

As children we are always daydreaming, creating, and thinking that everything's possible. We view the world as the canvas that we can shape, create, and make all our dreams come true. As children we remember why we came. Then we are taught to let go of our dreams and "keep our feet in the real world." We are taught that we must fit in a box in order to be successful. It's nothing but a robbery of passion and dreams.

Sometimes we realize, a little too late, that pursuing our dreams was really our true task to begin with. How many people do you think look back and regret not doing what they really wanted to do as children? Are you one of those people? We are here to be of service, to share our talents, to make others happy, and to create peace. Is your career choice doing these right now? How about reclaiming that creative child inside of you to lead you into living a life of fulfillment and joy?

You can do it! I believe it, do you?

Creativity- Week 22

Creativity is a type of learning process where the teacher and pupil are located in the same individual.
- Arthur Koestler

When our creativity is restricted we feel like something in our lives is missing. If we do not feed our creativity, it is like a part of us is dying. Since the universe is always changing, one can say that if you're not creating you are dying. Even if you just let your creative-self come out only "part time," it will really help you fulfill the dreams that you have been holding back.

Letting go of the expectations and the fears of acceptance by others while just being in the moment enjoying your creative side, can add years to your life; will bring back happiness, and will make you a better person. Dance, paint, play music, write, play a sport, garden, cook, bake, decorate, sew, and just do whatever it is that you like doing. It is imperative that YOU find the time to do the things that you love to do. Feed your spirit!

The world will be a better place once you start creating again.

Let's go!

Creativity- Week 23

Only creativity can see past problems to find solutions. This holds true for every area of life.
- *Deepak Chopra*

Creativity is the seed given to you by Your Source. It's the process where you share your life with this Source and Creator co-creating your world and your life together.

You are the creator of your life; you have the creativity to solve all the "problems" in your life and live the life of your dreams.

Creativity should be embraced and should also be shared. It is a part of you that makes you who you really are. It's a gift from your Creator which makes You also a Creator, since you are created in his image. What a wonderful gift! Can you see how fortunate you are?

Create your art; create your life; embrace it; share it; and be proud!

Creativity- Week 24

If you hear a voice within you say "You cannot paint," then by all means paint, & that voice will be silenced.
- *Vincent Van Gogh*

Not letting your desires be fulfilled because of a fear driven by the ego is the best way to make your life miserable and ultimately disappointing.

Creating your desires is your birthright; it is what you were meant to do! To do what brings you joy and a sense of accomplishment is why you came here. Do not let yourself get trapped by the rules of society in doing what's perceived as "the right and responsible thing to do."

You have a vision of what your life should be.

Hold on to that vision and start taking the first steps towards realizing your dreams. Miracles happen every single day. They're happening in your life right now. Embrace them and do what you love to do - then share it with the world.

We are all waiting!

Section 7

Health & Fitness

Health & Fitness- Week 25

A man's health can be judged by which he takes two at a time - pills or stairs.
- Joan Welsh

You are a spiritual being having a human experience.

You are the most amazing creation.

Do you believe that? If you do, then it's your responsibility to take care of your body and your health. Your body is the garage for your soul, and even though it's temporary, it is the temple that houses your magnificence.

Take pride in your body and health: feed it right, challenge it with exercise so it can have the energy and strength that's required for you to do your daily activities.

Stay healthy so you can enjoy life while sharing your life experience with your children, your family and others. Set a great example for your children and the rest of the world.

Health is only a decision away!

Health & Fitness- Week 26

A vigorous five-mile walk will do more good for an unhappy but otherwise healthy adult than all the medicine and psychology in the world.
- Paul Dudley

Exercise is as effective as medication in the treatment of depression and anxiety.

And you get even more rewards with exercise: a leaner and healthier body, which in turn will make you feel even better! Given the choice, would you choose pills and drugs versus just a natural high from exercise? Exercise makes you feel closer to your Source.

You cannot have a good quality of life if you are sick, achy, depressed, and anxious. Being happy and blissful is part of being healthy; and health is part of being able to exercise on a regular basis. Dr. Kenneth cooper said *"We do not stop exercising because we grow old - we grow old because we stop exercising."*

My question for you is: How OLD are you growing right now?

Health & Fitness- Week 27

Lack of activity destroys the good condition of every human being, while movement and methodical physical exercise save it and preserve it.
– Plato

Our Nation spends almost 3 trillion dollars a year in healthcare.

This is more than our Defense & Military Spending (7.5 billion) combined with Social Security (7.8 billion). This is the price that our whole nation is paying for disease and illnesses in our Country.

If you have a choice about being and staying healthy or sickness and illness, which one will you choose? The choice is available to you right now. Through exercise and proper nutrition most of our illnesses will disappear. Going back to placing value on things that money cannot buy, I ask you, how much is your health and quality of life worth to you?

Making the decision to move your body (exercise) and eating right can literally save and add quality years to your life. Are you in?

Health & Fitness- Week 28

***Your body is your most priceless possession;
you've got to take care of it!***
- Jack Lalanne

It's hard to feel happiness and bliss if you feel sick, depressed, without any energy, and feeling pain in your body. If you suffer from any of these, they can actually disappear from your body if you make the decision to take better care of yourself, exercise, and start eating properly.

Exercising is not about looking good; this is just a side effect. It's about taking care of your body temple - honoring and respecting yourself, while setting a great example for your children and the younger generation. It is about self-respect and becoming the best version of you.

Your body is not your soul, but it houses your spirit and you owe it to yourself and to your Creator to take good care of it. If you don't do it, who will?

This week try to get some exercise and some fresh air. Eat some fresh fruits and vegetables, while taking a little time just for you. You'll see that you'll feel refreshed, more energetic, more loving, and more tolerant of others.

Try it! I challenge you!

Section 8

Action

Action- Week 29

Do something. Whatever you do, it will be better than sitting and hoping things will improve.
– Robert Anthony

Hoping, wishful thinking, meditating, and praying are all great tools to help you advance your life towards your goals, unfortunately, without YOU taking the first step, absolutely nothing will change in your life.

Remember that your life is YOUR responsibility alone.

People blame their circumstances, their parents, their past, and their environment for being where they are, but until they take full responsibility, improvements will not be seen.

It is time to shed the cloak of blame and embrace action.

How can the universe know that you are committed to improving your life if you don't even take the first step? Haven't you dreamt enough? How about a reality check and a step towards your goals and your dream life?

It is time… Let's go!

Action- Week 30

An idea is a curious thing. It will not work unless you do.
– Jaeger's Facts

Everyone has creativity and passion. If you remember when you were a child, you surely remember being creative, day dreaming, and knowing what you were going to do when you grew up. Did those dreams change? Did you stop listening to the voice of creativity and dreams? Why? Would you believe it if I tell you that all the ideas and dreams you have had in your life are seeds that are waiting to germinate?

Your Creator has given you dreams and ideas that will only be realized if you believe in them - if you plant them, water & fertilize them and tend to them. Believe it because is true! Take one idea right now and take that first step to make it come true. You don't have to plan the whole thing, just take one step at a time. Like in a GPS, you have to enter your destination before you start moving towards it.

Decide what you want to do and take that first step. The timing is perfect! Trust in yourself and trust in the higher power that is helping you every step of the way.

Let's make that dream come true!

Action- Week 31

If you cannot do it today what makes you think you will do it tomorrow?
- Yusuf Tura

The timing for your ideas and dreams to start coming true is never "right" until you decide to take the first step.

Our society teaches us to wait "for the right time" and to "move cautiously" to "avoid disappointment and failure." I truly hope that this is not the way you are living your life right now because that is truly NOT living.

Taking risks, going after your dreams, and enjoying the ride (whether is scary or not), is the way you were meant to live. You came here to enjoy the contrast of everything that is available to you, yet, you try to avoid failure and disappointment at all costs.

Ask yourself, "What's the worst that can happen and can I live with it?" Tomorrow may not be here, but today is… Face your fears and go after your dreams.

This is YOUR life! Isn't it worth living to the fullest?

Action- Week 32

You miss 100% of the shots you don't take.
– Wayne Gretzky

Living a life full of regret and wishing for opportunities that came and passed because we didn't take any action is not a very pleasant place to be. Your future is determined right now.

Please think about this- <u>Everything that has happened in your life, has happened in the present.</u> We drag the baggage of the past around, but that past was once the present. We live in fear of what the future holds, but these things may never come to pass, so why ruin the present worrying?

Right now is all you have.

Forging your future the way you want it to be- the way you want to share it with your family, friends, and the world, starts right now. If not now, when? Remember, your life is an inspiration to others- how do you want to be remembered?

This is your call to action! I believe in you!
Starting today, let's forge your legacy; let's make your dreams come true!

Section 9

Abundance

Abundance- Week 33

Be generous! Give to those you love; give to those who love you; give to the fortunate; give to the unfortunate - yes, give especially to those you don't want to give. You will receive abundance for your giving. The more you give, the more you will have!
- W Clement Ston

Are you familiar with the Law of Cause and Effect? You are if you have heard any of these sayings: "As you sow, so shall you reap" "The more you give, the more you will receive" "What goes around comes around" "Whatever you do to others - will be done to you."

When you share your abundance (doesn't matter how much or how little), as long as you are sharing from the heart, the Universe rewards you three times as much as what you give. You will always win when you focus on giving. Giving is the cause of all abundance and prosperity.

TRUE giving and sharing comes from the heart and it has no expectations. Give yourself thoughts of abundance, prosperity, and wealth; and you shall receive that in return. Share your bounty with others because abundance is not ours, it's shared with us by the Universe, and we must continue sharing it with others.

What are you sharing and giving this week?

Abundance- Week 34

It's more work to create poverty, disease and disharmony than it is to create health, harmony and abundance, because perfect health, harmony and abundance are the natural order of things.
- Robert Anthony

If you can believe that Your Source created you and that you are a part of that Source and Creator; then, can you believe that abundance and prosperity are your natural state of being?

We have been led to believe a lie: that life is hard. We have been led to believe that lack and despair are natural states and that abundance and prosperity are only available to a few "lucky" ones. What if I told you that being poor, miserable, sick, scared, depressed, and anxious are states that YOU have chosen to be in? Can you believe that YOU alone have the power to change these conditions? We have been led to believe that we are separate from our Source, but this is not true. This separation is a mirage, an illusion that exists only in our minds.

My challenge for you this week is to make a choice to get out of these crazy conditions that are trapping you and preventing you from living your greatness. This week, dare to shine and be the star that you were meant to be. Your Source loves you and wants the best for you, why not embrace his gifts today?

Abundance- Week 35

There is no lack in the world. The lack is in you, and if you will stop seeking lack and stop thinking lack... you will make marvelous demonstrations.
- Al Koran

We live in an abundant and ever expanding Universe.

When you give, a vacuum is created and more comes to fill that space. Unfortunately, we have been programmed by society for competition and for lack. There's no shortage of resources and the economy is not collapsing.

Remember that by the Law of Attraction you get what YOU think about the most. If what occupies your mind is that you're living from paycheck to paycheck, that there's not going to be enough, that your job is not secure, that you will always struggle and be poor, then of course, that's exactly what your reality will be. By changing your thoughts and concentrating on how rich your life is right now - giving thanks for all the great things in your life - and knowing that everyday your life gets better and better, you will unlock the true potential of what's possible and available to you right now.

What do you say? Do you dare to pay more attention to abundance rather than lack?

I dare you...

Abundance- Week 36

When you realize there is nothing lacking, the whole world belongs to you.
- Lao Tzu

Let me help you remember something: Have you noticed that you always have what you need? I'm NOT talking about what you want… That's different! I'm talking about what you really need. Have you noticed that you always have what you need? Do you remember that going through the toughest times in your life was what helped you grow to the next level, to the next stage?

Learning to appreciate and give thanks for the tough times is what's needed to catapult you to the next stage of evolution and greatness in your life. Everything has a purpose - there's nothing wasted - and you always have exactly what you need. Like Bob Proctor says "You Were Born Rich." When you actually realize this truth and begin to see it every day in your life, the abundance and prosperity "will start" showing up. Being thankful now for everything that has been given to you puts you in a state of Grace.

Be aware of your abundance now and see how your life changes!

Section 10

Will Power

Will Power- Week 37

There can be no willpower without a dream to attach it to.
- Che Garman

One of the first questions I always ask is "What do you want?" You will be very surprised as to how many people are going through life right now without knowing what they want. How can the Universe help YOU get what you want to live the life of your dreams, if you don't even know what you want? It's like being in a car without a steering wheel: you'll go, but who knows where you'll end up and how many bumps and flips you'll do along the way.

You have the best GPS system at your disposal right now, however, without inputting the destination, where will you go, if any place at all? If you don't know exactly what you want, or where you want to be, now is the time to decide! If money was not a factor, what would you be doing right now?

What makes you happy?
Decide now and make the commitment to pursue your passion and happiness while adding value to the World. This is the first step to live the life of your dreams.

Are you ready? No excuses allowed!

Will Power- Week 38

Lack of willpower has caused more failure than lack of intelligence or ability.
- Flower A. Newhouse

Coaching athletes is something I did for over 30 years, and believe me when I tell you that a coach's nightmare is to have an athlete with all the talent in the world, without any passion or drive. The motivation and fire has to always come from within. I always said "I can't want it more than you do." The world is full of people with extraordinary talents and abilities who choose to let these abilities and talents go to waste because of laziness, lack of self-esteem, and fear.

Can you imagine being at your death bed and thinking, "Wow! I could've done so much but instead, I chose to do nothing!" How much regret do you think is in that statement? YOU have unique abilities and gifts given to you to share with the World.

Don't die with regrets and wishing "What if…" Starting today, invest your attention and your power in creating your dream life.

Take that first step to share YOUR talents with the World. You have kept us waiting long enough…

Will Power – Week 39

Do or do not... there is no try.
– Yoda

How many times we go through life saying "I'll try this; I'll try that," or better yet, "I tried but it didn't work out?" The thing about "trying" is that it gives you an out when you are not 100% committed. It's easy to say "I tried" and give up.

When there's a true intention and a true commitment there's no "try." When the fire burns inside of you and YOU want something so bad that sometimes it hurts, that's when there's "doing." That's where miracles happen and that's where the Universe will meet you three quarters of the way to help you accomplish your dreams.

When it comes to your dream life, your commitment to make this World a better place, YOUR legacy and YOUR inspiration to others, decide what those things are, and do them! There's no trying…

There's only Doing, so let's DO IT!

Will Power- Week 40

So many of our dreams at first seem impossible, then they seem improbable, and then when we summon the will, they soon become inevitable
- *Christopher Reeve*

Knowing what your dreams are and placing your attention in them will make them come true. Why? Because where ever you place your attention, you invest your energy, and this energy empowers your life

. Successful people place their attention in their dreams and in what they want to create for themselves and their families. They think about adding value to the World, about offering solutions to problems. This is how they become successful and earn a great living. Wouldn't you want to do the same? Start by offering a solution to a problem going on right now. Don't think of the money situation, just solve the problem. Help others help themselves - this way your success and financial reward will find their way back to you because of the value that you are adding to the World.

Your dreams can be YOUR reality. Take the first step towards this **commitment** and watch the magic happen!

My Year Of Inspiration

Section 11

Self Image

Self-Image- Week 41

Every man is the creation of himself, the image of his own thinking and believing.
- Claude M Bristol

Society teaches that we are what we do, our possessions, or reputations, and even our jobs. Does that sound reasonable to you? When was the last time you really thought about who YOU really are? When was the last time you thought about who YOU would like to BE?

Everything in our lives comes down to choices. You have the choice of being who you want to be today and every day. You are NOT - your mistakes, your failures, your bank account, your education, your job, or what you did or didn't do. Because YOU are a part of Your Source, YOU are a magnificent being who came forth into this world to share his/her gifts with others, to experience the deliciousness of contrast in this life, and to appreciate the opportunity of being here for a great adventure.

You didn't come here to live in lack and regret. Remember, feeling and being successful are just a choice away.

Stop playing small and believe in YOUR true greatness!

Self-Image- Week 42

It's not who you are that holds you back - it's who you think you're not!
– Unknown

The conditioning we receive as children stays with us for a lifetime if we let it.

It is time to shed the cloak of illusion and embrace our true selves! When we grow up we are conditioned to think that we are separate from everyone else, including our Source. We are taught lack and competition to keep this separation. Think about this for a second and realize how crazy this is! Yet, this separation is the cause of fear, suffering, and pain in our society. What we think we are is really a mask that was given to us at a young age and we have continued to wear it in fear of what society may think if we show our true selves.

You are not separate from your Source, you have NEVER been! As a glass of water from the ocean has all the qualities of the ocean, so do YOU, have all the qualities of Your Source because you were created in His/Her image. It's time to stop thinking separation and start thinking wholeness. Embrace your Source qualities and live them daily.

You can bring Heaven to Earth right now!

Self-Image- Week 43

Act the way you'd like to be and soon you'll be the way you act.
- Leonard Cohen

I keep talking about choices because I really want to drive the point home that in every single second of your life you have choices. These choices shape our lives but they don't have to define who we are. We are never stuck where we are. Because we are nothing but energy and energy is always changing, we are constantly changing.

If you feel stuck is because you keep your attention in being stuck.

Remember that you are your attention. When you start acting like the person you want to be, you become it because that's where your attention is. Have your attention in becoming the best husband, the best wife, the best son, the best daughter, the best at your job, the best neighbor, the best teacher, the best student, the best of who you are… Your attention is who you are today.

Who do you choose to be?

Self-Image- Week 44

At the moment when there's nothing more to lose, the Ego breaks open – and then we see who we are behind who we thought we were.
- *Baba Ram Dass*

Do you agree that adversity doesn't teach character, but it reveals it? When we are at our lowest points that is really when we find the strength and wisdom that we never thought we had. It is at the darkest times in our lives that we must seek the light and hold on to love. We need to be thankful and grateful for everything that comes into our lives, knowing that there are no accidents, and that we are ALWAYS where we are supposed to be.

Trusting that our lives are evolving and unfolding exactly the way that they are supposed to, we embrace changes, challenges and even "bad" times knowing that they are opportunities for growth and realization. Trusting in our Source is knowing that we are ALWAYS taken care of and ALWAYS have everything we truly need.

This is the week that your true character is revealed and when you take the first step towards YOUR BEST life yet.

Section 12

Opportunity

Opportunity- Week 45

Don't wait for extraordinary opportunities. Seize common occasions and make them great. Weak men wait for opportunities; strong men make them.
- Orison Swett Marden

How many people go through life saying "When opportunity comes I'll be ready" or "I'll know when is safe?" Ready or Safe for what? Life this time around is short and we didn't come here to "play it safe."

Remember that tomorrow is not promised to anyone so why not live this life to the fullest, embracing every opportunity that comes our way and even making new ones every day? There's never the "right time" to do something. The "right time" is when the idea comes to you and you take the first step to make it a reality. YOU make the "right time!" Is there something in your life you've wanted to do but have held back because is "not the right time?"

Dying tomorrow will make that wish a wasted wish because you never took the initiative and made the opportunity for its realization. How sad is that? Regrets? Let's not die with any! Seize the opportunities and if there's none, make them now!

What do you have to lose except living with regret?

Opportunity- Week 46

Effective people are not problem-minded; they're opportunity-minded. They feed opportunities and starve problems.
- Stephen Covey

Have you ever solved a problem by concentrating on the problem instead of the solution? No! It's impossible! You solve problems by concentrating on the solutions... So why so many people get stuck in their problems and they never want to come out? It gives them something to talk about. It gives them an excuse not to move forward. It may be because it gets them attention from others. Whatever the reason is, today YOU make the decision not to be one of those people!

Today is the day you decide that the drama in your life has come to an end and that opportunities are all you'll concentrate on from now on.

Excuses are no more! Starve that negativity baby!

Opportunity- Week 47

Too many people are thinking of security instead of opportunity. They seem more afraid of life than death.
- James F Bymes

Society teaches us to be afraid of the unknown. Like the unknown is something so bad... People stay in misery because they have become comfortable being miserable. It's familiar to them to be in their "comfort zone."

Make the decision today that you don't want to live in the worst room of this house. You want to live in the BEST room in this house. Period! Even if you don't know what it looks like, it cannot be any worse than the worst room, right?

Move out of the fear room and embrace the best room in the house, where opportunity, growth, and true living thrives. Remember, if you're not growing you are dying. That's the law. Stop reserving life today to die tomorrow.

What are you choosing today? Life, right?

Opportunity- Week 48

Each new day is a blank page in the diary of your life.
- *Douglas Pagels*

Taking responsibility for everything that happens in your life is scary at first, but then it becomes a true liberation. Knowing that everything in your life happened and happens because of YOUR choices, is like breathing fresh air for the first time. When you decide to go for your dream, no matter what obstacles (disguised opportunities) appear in your path, you become unstoppable.

The realization of your dream is YOUR responsibility, and YOURS alone. It's not your parents', your environment, your children's, or your spouse's responsibility.

To be happy now is YOUR decision.
Every single day is a blank page. What you decide to paint or write in that page is up to you. Decide to make it the best page in your life yet! How can it get any better than this? Wait and see, it's truly going to be great because YOU will make it great!

Section 13

Awareness

Awareness- Week 49

Every day we are engaged in a miracle which we don't even recognize: a blue sky, white clouds, green leaves, the black, curious eyes of a child -- our own two eyes. All is a miracle.
- *Thich Nhat Hanh*

The miracle of your own existence is something to be in awe of. Knowing that you are eternal, a part of Your Source - and the Source of everything else in the world - and that YOU too can create miracles, are some of the most amazing realizations.

YOU ARE indeed a true miracle!

The awareness of everything that has been created for you is what needs to be cultivated every day. Through your attention to everything that is, this awareness and delight will turn your experience into pure bliss. Realize that there's no moment more important than now. Realize that this moment is really all you have.

Embrace all that you are: truly magnificent! And enjoy every second of it!

Awareness- Week 50

Everything in your life is there as a vehicle for your transformation. Use it!
- Baba Ram Dass

Everything you need you already have.

This may not be everything you want, but everything you truly need. Realizing that there are no accidents and that every person you meet is here to help you realize your dreams, is very humbling. Knowing that the Universe revolves around you and is here to make all your wishes come true is the best way to start every single day. How wonderful is the fact that your life is YOUR creation (co-created with Your Source) and that surrendering to His/Her love is the BEST thing that you can experience?

It is said that "With God ALL things are possible." Does that leave ANYTHING out? ALL THINGS ARE possible with Your Creator! Do you believe this? Then, what are you waiting for?

Miracles in YOUR life are waiting to happen now. Let's make them come true!

Awareness- Week 51

Let your mind be quiet, realizing the beauty of the world, and the immense, the boundless treasures that it holds in store.
- Edward Carpenter

Our minds are hard to keep quiet. It is said that 'The average person has 60,000 thoughts per day and of these more than 80% are negative'. I hope that this doesn't apply to you, but if it does, know that YOU have the choice of keeping your attention in the negative thoughts or switching to the positive ones. It's the same effort, so why not choose positivity?

Remember the Law of Attraction? Like attracts like. Keeping your attention into positive thoughts will keep on bringing positive thoughts and positive experiences into your life. Meditation is a great way to connect directly to your Source and download wisdom instantly without the use of words. Meditation is a state of bliss that teaches you to surrender and appreciate everything that has been given to you.

This is a perfect week to quietly appreciate everything that is and to welcome in the quiet and the stillness. It's a beautiful world! Embrace it! Enjoy it!

Awareness- Week 52

Nothing is worth more than this day.
– Goethe

This is the week where everything comes together for you. This is when you realize that you cannot stop the negativity from going around, but you can prevent it from making a home in your mind. This is the week when you realize that you can turn into yourself to find YOUR true Source, your intuitive guidance, your wisdom, your joy, your peace and your love. You have had all these inside of you all along and looking for them outside makes absolutely no sense. This is the week when you co-create the rest of your life with your Source.

It is time to shine the light for others and to bring Heaven to Earth.

This is the week when you embrace your gifts, the essence of who you really are: an immortal being made of Love to share Love.

Today is the best day ever!

Nothing is worth more than this day, and it is yours to make the choices for your life. Embrace it!

Today, share your Greatness!

NOTES

My Year Of Inspiration

NOTES

My Daily & Weekly Journal

Week 1— Gratitude

Monday   **Date:** _____

Resistance Thoughts:

_____
_____
_____
_____

Positive Thoughts:

_____
_____
_____
_____

Today's Lesson

_____
_____
_____
_____
_____
_____
_____

My Year Of Inspiration

My Daily & Weekly Journal

Tuesday: Gratitude Date: _____

Resistance Thoughts:

_____
_____
_____
_____

Positive Thoughts:

_____
_____
_____
_____

Today's Lesson

_____
_____
_____
_____
_____
_____
_____

My Daily & Weekly Journal

Wednesday: Gratitude   Date: _____

Resistance Thoughts:

_____
_____
_____
_____

Positive Thoughts:

_____
_____
_____
_____

Today's Lesson

_____
_____
_____
_____
_____
_____

My Year Of Inspiration

My Daily & Weekly Journal

Thursday: Gratitude Date: _____

Resistance Thoughts:

_____
_____
_____
_____

Positive Thoughts:

_____
_____
_____
_____

Today's Lesson

_____
_____
_____
_____
_____
_____
_____

Willie Marrero-LaBonne

My Daily & Weekly Journal

Friday: Gratitude   Date: _____

Resistance Thoughts:

_____
_____
_____
_____

Positive Thoughts:

_____
_____
_____
_____

Today's Lesson

_____
_____
_____
_____
_____
_____
_____

My Daily & Weekly Journal

Saturday: Gratitude Date: _____

Resistance Thoughts:

_____
_____
_____
_____

Positive Thoughts:

_____
_____
_____
_____

Today's Lesson

_____
_____
_____
_____
_____
_____
_____

My Daily & Weekly Journal

Sunday: Gratitude   Date: _____

Resistance Thoughts:

_____
_____
_____
_____

Positive Thoughts:

_____
_____
_____
_____

Today's Lesson

_____
_____
_____
_____
_____
_____
_____

My Daily & Weekly Journal

My Week's Inspiration

ABOUT THE AUTHOR

Willie Marrero-LaBonne is a spiritual teacher, lightworker, and energy healer. She coached athletes of all disciplines for over 30 years on speed and agility teaching them how to find their confidence and greatness from within. She served in the US Army as a Counterintelligence Agent traveling all over the world speaking five languages. Willie is also a trained scientist as a Molecular Biologist and has dedicated her life to bridging science and spirit. She loves to open minds to the true reality, abundance, and creative power providing the training, tools, and the necessary information that can help transform lives. Willie lives in Wisconsin with her husband Jay, and her son, Brandon, who is also a writer.